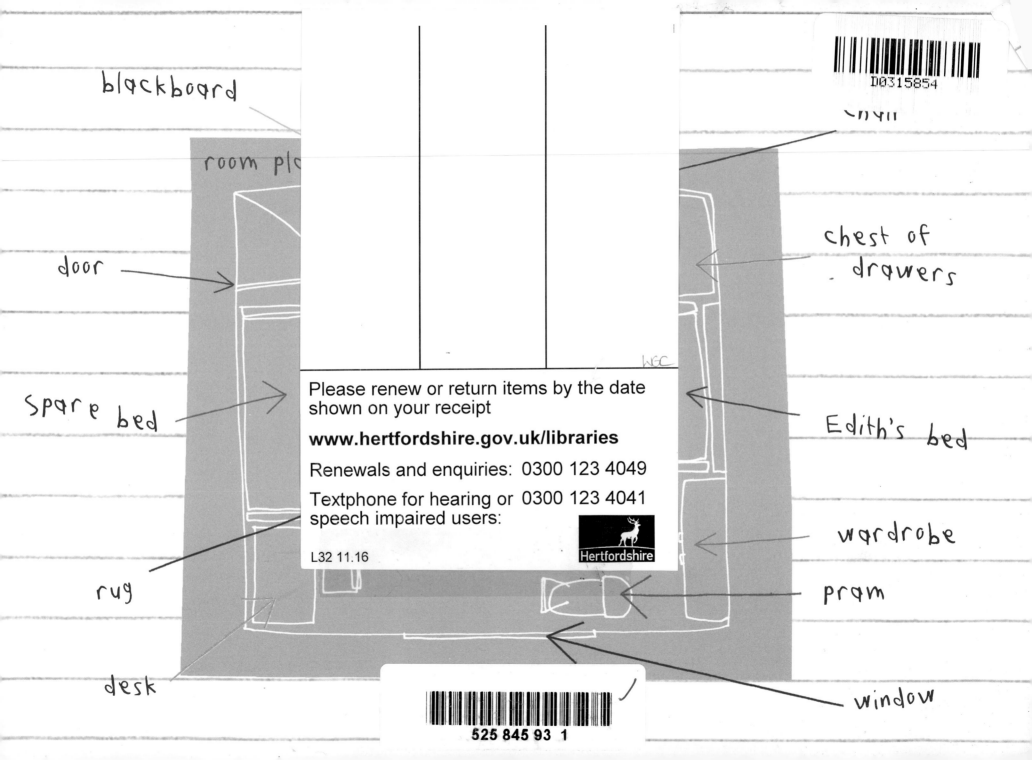

blackboard

room pla

door

chest of drawers

Spare bed

Edith's bed

wardrobe

rug

pram

desk

window

For Ada

First published in the United Kingdom in 2017 by
Pavilion Children's Books
43 Great Ormond Street
London
WC1N 3HZ

An imprint of Pavilion Books Company Limited

ISBN: 9781843653271

A CIP catalogue record for this book is available from the British Library.

10 9 8 7 6 5 4 3 2 1

Reproduction by Mission, Hong Kong
Printed by Toppan Leefung Printing Ltd, China

This book can be ordered directly from the publisher online at
www.pavilionbooks.com, or try your local bookshop.

My new room

by lisa stickley

My name is Edith. I am little.
I am bigger than I was last year, but
not as big as I will be next year.

Last month, on a Wednesday, I moved
into my new room, along with
all my toys.

Gary Guardsman is settled on the bookshelf.

"As head of moving and room safety, I have been keeping everyone in check to ensure a smooth and safe move."

Albert now lives at the bottom
of Edith's bed.

"It's usually ok smelly wise as most nights
Edith has a bath, so her feet aren't
like stink bombs!" says Albert.

Osbert T. Octopus resides on top of a bright blue chest of drawers.

"They are almost the same colour as my stripes, which makes me feel extremely special, because we match," whispers Osbert.

Tony Sloth likes snoozing on the spare bed, next to Reginald Rabbit.

"The bed is sometimes used by Grandma when she stays over. It is an extremely HUGE and spacious place to sleep. It is big enough for Reginald's ears too, which are GINORMOUS!" giggles Tony.

"Humph," replies Reginald, "don't be so cheeky."

A PLATE FOR THE
plaice

S P

Major Ted now lives on Edith's pillow.

"My duties include bed-making patrol, spider removal and bad dream soothing.

"I sometimes have to wear earplugs to block out Edith's snoring, but that's just part of the job," pronounces Ted.

Margot the cat sits on the chair, next to the blackboard.

"It is on the warmer side of the room, which is preferable for me, but the chalk dust plays havoc with my allergies.

"I am keeping my eyes peeled for an alternative position," purrs Margot.

Clarissa the Cow is enjoying her new home on the desk.

"I am entertaining EVERYONE with my tap dancing. Being wooden on a wooden desk means I make a FANTASTIC NOISE. The BEST EVER.

"I think Margot and Tony particularly like it, as they hold their hands up to their ears in DELIGHT," moos Clarissa.

Susan, Maurice and Mr Rabbit
take pride of place on the wardrobe.

"It's great," says Maurice.

"I hide on the door knob, camouflaged.
Only Edith knows I'm here!"

From the top of the wardrobe,
Mr Rabbit proudly states," the view of
the garden from up here is marvellous."

"And I can indulge in my secret love
of plane spotting," says Susan,
beaming broadly.

Breton Mouse sits on the mushroom pouffe in the middle of the rug.

"I can practise trampolining as the mushroom is extremely boingy. The rug is a great landing spot if I somersault on a slight wonk," bellows Breton.

Bartholomew lives in the toy pram.

"Oh yes, it's very cosy in here and it suits my hibernating tendencies very well.

"When Edith pushes the pram on the carpet it jiggles and tickles," titters Bartholomew.

Sebastian is positioned at the bottom of the door.

"Being a draft excluder, the position comes with the profession. I don't mind when push comes to shove, but I do find it a bit chilly.

"If I could just coil myself round a bit, I could be a floor cushion instead, on the big warm rug.

"I might apply for a promotion,"
shivers Sebastian.

One to ten

"Good work, team! All in all I think we have done very well settling in," declares Gary.

"Yes, I think we might like it here.

"Quiet everyone! Here comes Edith!"

"Ooh, I love my new room too, but I wonder who put that banner there," ponders Edith.